THE
LEGEND
OF
MICHAEL
JORDAN

Fountaindale Public Library
Bolingbrook, IL
(630) 759-2102

D1405949

TRIUMPH
BOOKS

Copyright © 2020 by Triumph Books LLC

No part of this publication may be reproduced, stored in a retrieval system, or transmitted in any form by any means, electronic, mechanical, photocopying, or otherwise, without the prior written permission of the publisher, Triumph Books LLC, 814 North Franklin Street, Chicago, Illinois 60610.

Library of Congress Cataloguing-in-Publication Data available upon request

This book is available in quantity at special discounts for your group or organization. For further information, contact:

Triumph Books LLC
814 North Franklin Street
Chicago, Illinois 60610
(312) 337-0747
www.triumphbooks.com

Printed in U.S.A.

ISBN: 978-1-62937-865-7

Content written, developed, and packaged by Adam Motin
Design and page production by Patricia Frey
Cover design by Preston Pisellini

Photos on pages 1, 9, 27, 31, 36, 45, 48, 51, 52, 58, 62, 64, 69, 73, 79, 85, 92, 95, 104, 106, 109, 110, and 112 courtesy of AP Images; 5, 6, 9, and 70 courtesy of USA Today Network; 10, 12, 15, 16, 20, 24, 28, 32, 39, 42, 54, 57, 67, 75, 86, 88, 91, 96, 98, 100, and 103 courtesy of Getty Images; 19, 22, 35, 40, 46, 61, 76, 80, and 83 courtesy of Newscom. Illustrations by iStock.

This is an unofficial publication. This book is in no way affiliated with, licensed by, or endorsed by Michael Jordan, the National Basketball Association, or any associated entities.

INTRODUCTION

In the world of basketball, Michael Jordan is the G.O.A.T.

The. Greatest. Of. All. Time.

Need proof? A national championship in college. Two Olympic gold medals. Six NBA championships, including two three-peats and six Finals MVP awards. Slam dunk champion. Scoring titles. The Shot. The Shrug. The Flu Game.

But MJ was also so much more.

Michael changed the way we think about basketball and turned it into one of the world's most popular sports. He made collecting sneakers cool and changed pop culture forever. He dominated the NBA on the court, left to follow a boyhood dream, then returned and dominated *again*. He became the first former player to own an NBA team. He also starred in a hit movie with Bugs Bunny!

The following pages look back on MJ's incredible life and career, from his earliest days playing the game he loved to his unforgettable final shot with the Chicago Bulls to his current status as an American icon.

THE LEGEND BEGINS

Michael Jeffrey Jordan was born on February 17, 1963. Despite spending most of his childhood in Wilmington, North Carolina, Michael was actually born in Brooklyn, New York, an area where he'd stage some of his most thrilling moments on the court decades later. His parents, James and Deloris, were in Brooklyn for just 18 months while James was studying airplane hydraulics.

As a newborn, Michael was kept in the hospital for several days for observation. The family had another scare several years later when he was shocked after touching a live electrical wire.

"I've got to believe one thing," James Jordan told the *Chicago Tribune*. "One day, God was sitting around and decided to make the perfect basketball player. He gave him a little hardship early to make him appreciate what he would earn in the end and called him Michael Jordan."

Michael was interested in sports from a young age, and his first love was baseball, not basketball. Perhaps he wanted to follow in his father's footsteps; James had been a semipro player in his younger days. Thankfully for the rest of us, eventually Michael found the game of basketball.

A FAMILY AFFAIR

James and Deloris had five children in all: Ronnie, Deloris, Larry, Michael, and Roslyn. The Jordans were a close family, and Michael credits much of his competitive spirit to playing countless games against his brothers, particularly Larry.

"We had this barbecue pit that we'd use as the backstop, and we'd play baseball with a tennis ball, and we had numerous battles," Larry told ESPN. "If I lost, I had to keep playing until I won. That's why, more often than not, it would end in a fight."

"I don't think from a competitive standpoint, I would be here without the confrontations with my brother," Michael said in *The Last Dance* documentary. "When you come to blows with someone you absolutely love, that's igniting every fire within you. And I always felt I was fighting Larry for my father's attention."

Of all the Jordans, no one was closer than Michael and his father. The two were often inseparable during MJ's career with the Chicago Bulls.

"My heroes were and are my parents. I can't see myself having anyone else as my heroes," Michael once said.

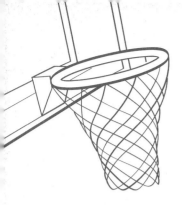

MICHAEL JORDAN GOT CUT... OR DID HE?

One of the most famous and often-repeated stories from Michael's younger days was that he was "cut" from the Laney High School basketball team. Michael himself has repeated the tale, admitting that he went home and cried when he heard the news. The story is seen as an early example of his ability to turn someone doubting him into the motivation that fueled his greatness.

But did it really happen? Was Michael Jordan not "good enough" to make his high school basketball team? The truth is, not exactly.

Michael wasn't actually "cut" from the team; as a sophomore, he was placed on the JV squad, rather than the varsity team. As the coach, Clifton "Pop" Herring, explained to *Sports Illustrated*, it was rare for a sophomore to make the varsity roster, and the only one who did was 6-foot-7, much taller than the 5-foot-11 Michael.

Michael joined the varsity for his junior and senior years and was an instant star, averaging 27 points, 12 rebounds, and six assists per game in his final season. Sometimes good things come to those who wait!

MICHAEL GOES TO CHAPEL HILL

When it came time to choose a college, Michael considered UCLA, a school that had many dominant teams during his childhood, and Virginia, home to star Ralph Sampson. But in the end he decided to stay close to home and play for the legendary Dean Smith at North Carolina.

It proved to be a wise decision.

As a freshman, the player known by many as "Mike Jordan" averaged 13.4 points per game and was named the conference's Freshman of the Year. In Coach Smith's team-oriented offense, it was hard for any one player to dominate the score sheet; in coming years, it would be joked that the only person who could hold MJ under 20 points was Dean Smith. But even he couldn't keep Michael from playing the hero.

At the end of his freshman season, with the Tar Heels trailing the Georgetown Hoyas by one point in the final seconds of the NCAA national championship game, Michael connected on a game-winning jump shot to give Smith the first title of his storied career.

It was also just the first in a long line of unforgettable moments courtesy of Michael Jordan.

"[My career] would've never happened without Coach Smith."

—Michael Jordan

ranville Tower
UNIVERSITY SQUARE
APEL HILL, NC 27514
hael Jordan
035

THE GREATEST NBA DRAFT EVER

After being named an All-American the next two years and winning the College Player of the Year award in his junior year, Michael decided to enter the 1984 NBA Draft. It was a star-studded class at the time that has only become more famous—and infamous—over the years.

Everyone agreed that the first overall pick, owned by the Houston Rockets, would be local college standout Hakeem Olajuwon, a dynamic center at a time when size still mattered in the NBA. The Portland Trail Blazers held the second pick, and with guard Clyde Drexler already on their roster, they chose Kentucky center Sam Bowie over MJ.

It turned out to be the worst pick of all time.

The Chicago Bulls gladly selected Michael with the third overall pick, and the rest is history.

Four of the players from the 1984 draft were named to the league's list of its 50 greatest players: Olajuwon, Jordan, Charles Barkley, and John Stockton. Many other fine players were selected, including Sam Perkins, Alvin Robertson, and Otis Thorpe. Unfortunately for both Sam Bowie and Portland, his name became synonymous with things going wrong on draft night.

BUT FIRST, OLYMPIC GOLD

Before putting on his famous number 23 Bulls jersey, Michael first wore a number 9 jersey for Team USA at the 1984 Summer Olympics.

Coached by Indiana's fiery Bobby Knight and blessed with great college players including MJ, Patrick Ewing, Wayman Tisdale, and Chris Mullin, Team USA went undefeated in the tournament and won the gold medal. Michael led the team in scoring and dazzled a global audience with the breathtaking athleticism he wasn't always able to showcase at North Carolina. Certainly he'd turned his Olympic coach into a believer.

"If I were going to pick the three or four best athletes I've ever seen play basketball, he'd be one of them. I think he's the best athlete I've ever seen play basketball, bar none," Knight said. "If I were going to pick people with the best ability I've ever seen play the game, he'd be one of them. If I wanted to pick one of the best competitors, he'd be one of them. He's the best athlete, he's one of the best competitors, he's one of the most skilled players, and that to me makes him the best basketball player I've ever seen play."

A ROAR
IN CHICAGO

MJ wasted no time in setting the NBA world on fire.

Michael averaged an astonishing 28.2 points per game on 51.5 percent shooting on his way to winning the Rookie of the Year award. The Bulls, who had barely won a third of their games the previous three seasons, were suddenly must-watch TV and playoff contenders. Opposing fans cheered Michael when he came to town, and they rewarded him with a starting spot in that season's All-Star Game. He graced the cover of *Sports Illustrated* that December under the headline, "A Star Is Born." He scored more than 40 points seven times, including 49 points against Detroit in February.

Still, all was not perfect. The Bulls were short on talent, and though they made a return to the playoffs, they were swept in the first round. Plus, MJ's first All-Star Game appearance was spoiled by what he considered a conspiracy, led by the Pistons' Isiah Thomas, to prevent him from touching the basketball. It would be the first of many battles between Michael and the "Bad Boys" from Detroit.

"There is no 'i' in 'team' but there is in 'win.'"

—Michael Jordan

IT'S GOTTA BE THE SHOES!

It may be hard to imagine the worlds of basketball, sneakers, and pop culture before the Air Jordan 1.

Yes, some NBA players endorsed sneakers, but many companies thought that endorsements from players in team sports wasn't always a good investment. The notion of collectible sneakers, or waiting in long lines to purchase them, was foreign. Nike was known largely as a running shoe company that couldn't compete with the likes of Reebok.

Then again, no one had ever seen anything like Michael Jordan or his iconic signature shoe before.

After signing MJ to the richest shoe contract in history, Nike released the Air Jordan 1 to coincide with Michael's rookie season. The high-cut shoes were made of individual pieces in different colors, unlike most basketball shoes of the day, and featured the first "Jumpman" logo, today one of the most famous logos on the planet.

Nike hoped to sell 100,000 pairs in that first year. Instead, the company shipped out 1.5 million pairs in the first six weeks.

Today, the AJ1 is still the most popular sneaker in the world, helping propel the Jordan Brand to $3.1 billion in sales in 2019. Much like the man for whom they are named, they are the G.O.A.T.

"It's not about the shoes, it's what you do in them."

—Michael Jordan

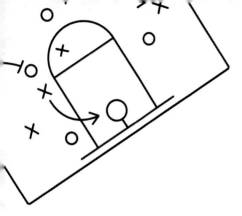

A BUMP IN THE ROAD

Hopes were high in Chicago entering the 1985 NBA season. Unfortunately for the fans, the Bulls, and MJ, they were about to crash back to earth.

In just the third game of the year, against Golden State, MJ came down hard on his left foot and broke a bone. The injury would keep him out for the next 64 games.

For someone like Michael who lived to compete, sitting out month after month was agonizing. Things only got worse when doctors advised the Bulls there was a 10 percent chance MJ could suffer a career-ending injury if he came back too soon. The team wanted Michael to sit out the rest of the season and the playoffs.

Michael refused.

"I think people were just being conservative," MJ said at the time. "The doctors say that the bone hasn't completely healed, but to wait for that would mean a year, maybe a year and a half."

Michael went back to North Carolina, where he participated in drills and played games without informing the Bulls. He convinced the Bulls to let him return to play in the postseason against the legendary Boston Celtics. He was about to make history, again.

10

"GOD DISGUISED AS MICHAEL JORDAN"

The eighth-seeded Bulls had no chance of beating the top-seeded Boston Celtics in the 1986 postseason. The Celtics had Larry Bird, Kevin McHale, Robert Parish, and all those championship banners hanging in Boston Garden. Most believed the Bulls should have been happy to make the playoffs after losing MJ for most of the regular season.

Apparently, no one told Michael Jordan.

After scoring 49 points in a Game 1 loss, MJ set the all-time playoff scoring record with 63 points in a double-overtime loss in Game 2.

"He is the most awesome player in the NBA," Bird said. "Today in Boston Garden, on national TV, in the playoffs, he put on one of the greatest shows of all time. I couldn't believe anybody could do that against the Boston Celtics."

MJ finished 22 of 41 from the field and 19 of 21 from the free-throw line, to go along with six assists and five rebounds. It was an incredible performance from a second-year pro and remains one of the greatest playoff games in league history.

"I would never have called him the greatest player I'd ever seen if I didn't mean it," Bird told the *Boston Globe*. "It's just God disguised as Michael Jordan."

YOU'LL BELIEVE A MAN CAN FLY

Michael Jordan has become synonymous with the slam dunk and the NBA's Slam Dunk Contest, but the truth is he didn't invent either.

Players with the skills to do so were dunking back in the 1940s, and college basketball even outlawed the dunk from 1967 to 1976, largely because of the dominance of center Lew Alcindor. But fans and players alike loved the dunk, and by 1984 the NBA had made the dunk contest a part of All-Star Weekend.

MJ's first appearance came in 1985, where he lost to Atlanta's Dominique Wilkins in the final round, despite Michael throwing one down after taking off from the free-throw line. MJ skipped the next year's contest, but then cemented his place in dunk history by winning back-to-back titles in 1987 and 1988. The battle between MJ and Wilkins in 1988, in front of a packed Chicago Stadium, is still remembered as the greatest dunk contest in history. MJ again dunked from the free-throw line, a moment captured in one of the most iconic basketball photographs of all time. It was a fitting tribute to the man who made the slam dunk his own.

HELP ARRIVES FROM ARKANSAS

Despite Michael's heroics—in 1986, he became only the second player in league history to score 3,000 points in a season, averaging an NBA-best 37.1 points per game—the Bulls struggled to build a championship team around him. That began to change in 1987, when they found the help they needed in the most unlikeliest of places: Conway, Arkansas.

Scottie Pippen was a skinny small forward with great potential, but playing for the University of Central Arkansas hadn't given him much experience against top-flight competition. But after acquiring him on draft night, along with power forward Horace Grant, the Bulls' fortunes began to change. Scottie quickly became the perfect partner to MJ, playing incredible defense and taking some of the burden off of Michael on offense.

Still, few could have imagined back in 1987 that Michael and Scottie would go down in NBA history as one of the most successful duos of all time, winning six championships together.

"Whenever they speak Michael Jordan, they should speak Scottie Pippen," MJ said in *The Last Dance*. "When everybody says, well, I won all these championships—but I didn't win without Scottie Pippen. And that's why I consider him my best teammate of all time."

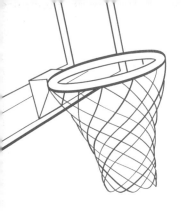

THE SHOT

One sign of MJ's greatness is how many of his unforgettable moments can be referred to by a simple phrase. Perhaps the first one in his NBA career came on May 7, 1989, in Game 5 of a first-round playoff series against the Cleveland Cavaliers. It is known simply as "The Shot."

The third-seeded Cavs had gone 6–0 against the sixth-seeded Bulls during the regular season, but MJ and the Bulls pushed them to a deciding fifth game in Cleveland during this series. The game seesawed down to the final minute, with the lead changing hands six times in 60 seconds.

MJ's jump shot with six seconds left gave the Bulls the lead, but the Cavs' Craig Ehlo converted a layup three seconds later. The scene was set for Michael to drag Ehlo with him into immortality.

The Bulls' Brad Sellers inbounded the ball to MJ, who was being double-teamed by Larry Nance and Ehlo. Michael dribbled to the foul line and jumped, as did Ehlo. But MJ hung in the air long enough to get a clean look at the basket, and his shot was true. The Bulls had won. The Shot had been made.

The image of Michael leaping in the air and pumping his fist is known to all basketball fans. He would create many more moments like it in the years to come.

ENTER THE ZEN MASTER

The Bulls seemed ready to take the next step toward a championship, but the team felt head coach Doug Collins had taken them as far as he could. A change of leadership was needed.

Much like the acquisition of Scottie Pippen in 1987, the promotion of Phil Jackson to head coach in 1989 came with high risk and possibly great rewards. A champion as a player with the New York Knicks, Phil had never been a head coach in the NBA before. Later nicknamed "The Zen Master" because of his philosophical approach to the game, he also was a fan of the Triangle offense, a scheme that emphasized ball movement and an equal distribution of opportunities. Some wondered if that type of coach would be a good fit for a fearless scorer like MJ, including Michael himself.

"I wasn't a Phil Jackson fan when he first came in…because he was coming in to take the ball out of my hands," Michael said.

Time would prove that the partnership between Phil and MJ was a match made in heaven. But their road to the top would have to go through Detroit.

MJ VS. THE BAD BOYS

The Detroit Pistons were the best team in the Eastern Conference, and they weren't interested in making room for MJ and the Bulls.

After losing to the Los Angeles Lakers in the 1988 NBA Finals, the Pistons had won back-to-back titles in 1989 and 1990. Led by point guard Isiah Thomas and coach Chuck Daly, the team combined smart play and tough defense into a recipe for success.

For three straight seasons, beginning in 1987–88, the two teams met in the playoffs with the Pistons winning each series. Part of their success was due to the "Jordan Rules," a defensive "scheme" that amounted to little more than cheap shots and dirty plays. It was effective, though, at least for a while.

By 1991, MJ and the Bulls had learned their lessons and Detroit's time had come. The Bulls destroyed their rivals in a four-game sweep, after which a humiliated Thomas led his teammates off the court before the game was over or congratulatory handshakes could be given. It was a fitting end to the Pistons' reign.

After the series, MJ said, "You see two different styles with us and them. The dirty play and the flagrant fouls and unsportsmanlike conduct, hopefully, that will be eliminated from the game…But I haven't agreed with the methods they used. I think people are happy the game will get back to a clean game and away from the 'Bad Boy' image."

"I can accept failure; everyone fails at something. But I can't accept not trying."

—Michael Jordan

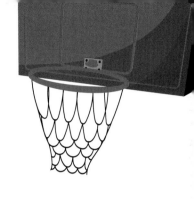

AT LAST!

For years, doubts had surrounded Michael Jordan: could a roster built around a player who scored so many points succeed in the playoffs? Could the league's leading scorer lead his team to a championship?

In 1991, MJ was finally able to erase all doubts.

During the regular season, MJ averaged 31.5 points per game and won his second MVP award. Scottie Pippen had become an All-Star, and the supporting cast was ready to win. After tearing through the Eastern Conference, only one obstacle remained: Magic Johnson and the legendary Lakers.

In the end, it was no contest. The Bulls lost Game 1 at home but then swept the next four for their first championship in franchise history. Perhaps the most memorable moment came in Game 2, when Michael took off toward the basket with the ball in his outstretched right arm, then switched the ball to his left hand in midair before laying it in. Announcer Marv Albert famously shouted, "A spectacular move by Michael Jordan!" Later, MJ said, "It wasn't even one of my best creative shots."

Michael was predictably awarded the Finals MVP award, the first of many. He was finally a champion.

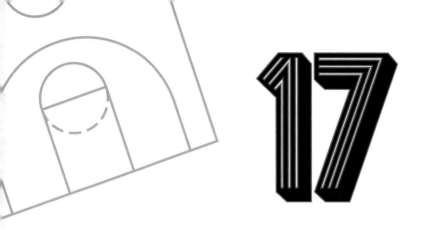

BE LIKE MIKE

By 1991, MJ had become one of the biggest celebrities in the world. In addition to his performance on the court, he had also become a superstar in commercials, endorsing products for Nike, Hanes, Coca-Cola, McDonald's, and Chevrolet. Coming off his first NBA championship with the Bulls, Gatorade signed Michael to be the company's first and only celebrity spokesperson, then released one of the most memorable commercial campaigns of all time.

The "Be Like Mike" ad featured clips of Michael in action on the court and footage of kids on the playground trying to copy his moves. But it was the catchy tune and lyrics that made the spot unforgettable:

> Sometimes I dream / That he is me
> You've got to see that's how I dream to be
> I dream I move, I dream I groove
> Like Mike
> If I could Be Like Mike

In 2016, *USA Today* ranked the "Be Like Mike" ad the greatest sports commercial of all time.

THE SHRUG

MJ and the Bulls returned to the NBA Finals in 1992, with the media and the fans asking two big questions: could the team win back-to-back titles, and was Michael really that much better than Clyde Drexler, the star guard of the Portland Trail Blazers?

Never someone who needed extra motivation, MJ answered those questions in the first half of Game 1.

Looking for every opportunity to go after Drexler, Michael scored 35 points in that first half, including a Finals-record six three-pointers. After hitting his final three, he turned toward the sideline and shrugged his shoulders, admitting that even he couldn't believe how good he was. The moment has become known as "The Shrug."

In *The Last Dance*, Michael said, "Clyde was a threat. I'm not saying he wasn't a threat, but me being compared to him, I took offense to that."

Things didn't get much better for Drexler or the Blazers, as the Bulls won their second championship, this time in six games.

"Obstacles don't have to stop you. If you run into a wall, don't turn around and give up. Figure out how to climb it, go through it, or work around it."

—Michael Jordan

19

THE DREAM TEAM

Just when it seemed MJ couldn't become any more popular, it was time for the 1992 Summer Olympics held in Barcelona, Spain.

For the first time, the United States sent professionals from the NBA instead of college players. Nicknamed "The Dream Team," it was the greatest collection of basketball talent ever assembled, and perhaps the greatest in any sport. Among the players selected were Magic Johnson, Larry Bird, Charles Barkley, Scottie Pippen, and, of course, MJ, the biggest star among stars.

The team was treated like royalty everywhere they went; thousands of people surrounded their hotel just to get a glimpse of their heroes. Despite beating their opponents by an average of 44 points on their way to the gold medal, MJ and the Dream Team are largely credited with turning basketball into a truly global sport. In 1991, there were 23 international players in the NBA; in 2019, that number was 108 and included some of the best players in the game, such as Giannis Antetokounmpo, Luka Doncic, and Joel Embiid.

20

THREE-PEAT!

MJ had one goal going into the 1993 season: winning the Bulls' third straight championship, something legends Magic Johnson and Larry Bird had been unable to accomplish in their careers. Standing in his way was his old friend and Dream Team teammate, Charles Barkley, and the Phoenix Suns. Despite scoring 32.6 points per game during the regular season and finishing second in Defensive Player of the Year award voting, Michael lost the MVP award to Barkley, providing even more fuel for MJ's fire.

Michael averaged a Finals-record 41 points per game during the series, which the Bulls won thanks to a game-winning shot by John Paxson in Game 6. MJ won his third straight Finals MVP award, and his greatness had become so predictable that some fans thought there was nothing he could do to surprise them.

He was about to prove them wrong.

> **"The one thing I do know is my heart, my soul, my love has always gone to the city of Chicago."**
>
> —Michael Jordan

MICHAEL SHOCKS THE WORLD

The Chicago White Sox were playing the Toronto Blue Jays in a playoff game on October 5, 1993, when a rumor began circulating through Comiskey Park: Michael Jordan, who was on hand to throw out the ceremonial first pitch, was planning to retire from the NBA the following morning.

It was hard to believe; the Bulls had just completed the three-peat and MJ was in his prime at the age of 30. He was the most popular athlete in the world. How could he just walk away?

Surrounded by his teammates, family and friends, and dozens of reporters, Michael said, "I've always stressed to people that have known me and the media that has followed me that when I lose the sense of motivation and the sense to prove something as a basketball player, it's time for me to move away from the game of basketball...But I just feel that I don't have anything else for myself to prove."

The announcement shocked the NBA and the world at large. The greatest player in the game was walking away. What no one could've guessed was that he would soon walk toward another sport.

MEET THE JORDANS

Michael had proven to be so many things: a national champion. Two-time Olympic gold medalist. Three-time NBA champion and Finals MVP. But he is also a husband and father.

MJ married his wife, Juanita, in 1989, and the couple had three children: sons Jeffrey and Marcus, and daughter Jasmine. Juanita was insistent that the kids learned to stand on their own two feet.

"The coaches always wanted them to wear the number 23 because their dad was number 23, but it was important to me that they learn not to try to be their dad," Juanita told *Crain's Chicago Business* in 2013. "They had to develop their own skills and they needed to work hard and learn how to manage their own challenges...Living in suburbs was a life that they got to enjoy because of their wealth. However, it was important to me that they also experienced how I grew up...They saw how people on the south side of Chicago who didn't have as much as they did, they saw how they lived and what the real world was about."

Michael and Juanita separated in 2006. MJ remarried in 2013, and he and his wife, Yvette Prieto, have twin daughters, Victoria and Ysabel.

MICHAEL JORDAN, OUTFIELDER

Four months after retiring at the height of his career, Michael Jordan, the world's greatest basketball player, announced that he was going to become a professional baseball player.

Wait, *what*?

Hard as it is to believe, MJ decided to follow a boyhood dream he shared with his late father and try to play Major League Baseball. After signing a minor league contract with the White Sox, Michael rode on buses with the Double-A Birmingham Barons, batting .202 with three home runs, 51 RBIs, and 30 stolen bases, a remarkable performance considering he hadn't played baseball since he was a teenager. His manager, future World Series winner Terry Francona, was a believer.

"He had it all," Francona told ESPN. "Ability, aptitude, work ethic...I do think with another 1,000 at-bats, he would've made it. But there's something else that people miss about that season. Baseball wasn't the only thing he picked up. I truly believe that he rediscovered himself, his joy for competition."

A players' strike cut the 1994 baseball season short and made it unlikely MJ would have time to reach the majors. He would need to find another way to display his "joy for competition."

"My father used to say that it's never too late to do anything you wanted to do. And he said you never know what you can accomplish until you try."

—Michael Jordan

MICHAEL JORDAN

CHICAGO BULLS
1984 — 1993

there ever was. The best there ever will be

DEDICATED
NOVEMBER 1, 1994

CAST IN BRONZE

With Michael retired from basketball, the time seemed right to dedicate a statue outside the United Center, the Bulls' home that has often been referred to as "The House That Michael Built."

On November 1, 1994, that statue was unveiled in front of MJ, his family, and a national TV audience. The piece, which measures 17 feet tall and weighs 2,000 pounds, depicts Michael in his iconic Jumpman pose. Inscribed along with MJ's achievements are the words, "The best there ever was. The best there ever will be."

The statue became an immediate tourist attraction in Chicago.

"It's mind-blowing," Steve Schanwald, the Bulls' executive vice president of business operations, told the *Chicago Tribune* in 2009. "I don't care what time you leave this building, someone will be there, taking a picture."

The statue now resides within the United Center atrium but is still accessible to fans.

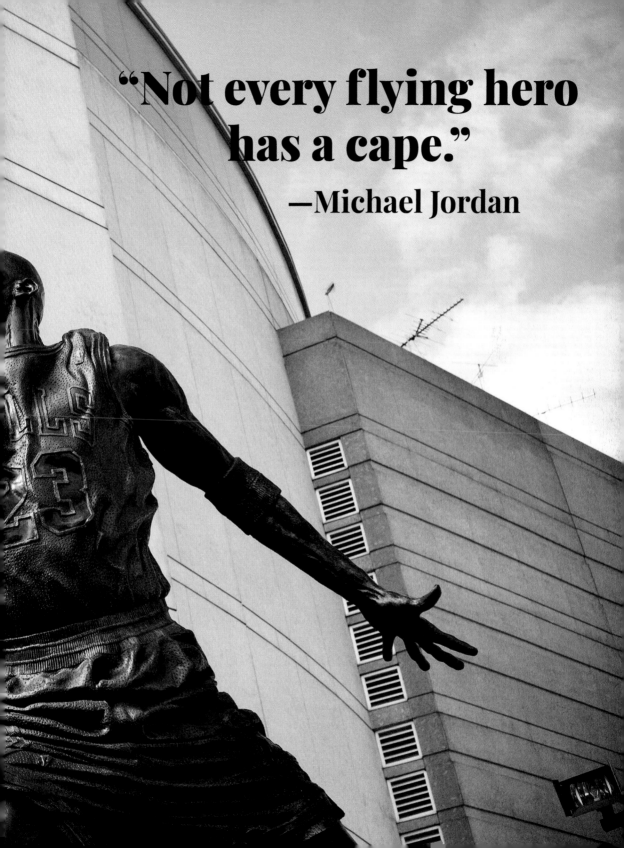

"Not every flying hero has a cape."

—Michael Jordan

"I'M BACK"

Teammate Toni Kukoc estimated that after he retired, MJ showed up at the Bulls practice facility to work out or play basketball about once a month. But during the first week of March of 1995, there were numerous sightings of Michael and rumors of him preparing for a return to basketball.

The city of Chicago broke into a frenzy. Could it be? Was Michael coming back to the Bulls?

Finally, on March 18, the world got the answer it had hoped for. After his agent wrote several versions of a press release, MJ put them aside and released a two-word statement of his own: "I'm back."

In addition to acknowledging he may have been burned out in 1993, coach Phil Jackson had another theory behind MJ's comeback.

"I always thought he might think that no one had ever returned from retirement before, and that he could lead a team to a championship again, win another scoring title after retiring," Jackson told NBA reporter Sam Smith. "That's something he could want to do."

Seventeen months after retiring, the G.O.A.T. was back.

26

WHAT'S IN A NUMBER?

The number 23 has become synonymous with Michael Jordan. But that's not the only number he wore during his career.

First things first: legend has it that MJ wore 23 starting in high school because his brother Larry wore number 45, so the younger Michael divided 45 in half and rounded up. In his two Olympic appearances, where numbers are assigned 1 through 15, Michael wore 9, which was the sum of 4 and 5.

Michael wore 45 during his time in baseball, and also wore it after his return to basketball in 1995, saying it represented a new start. But before too long, he reclaimed the famous number 23.

There is one more number that only the biggest MJ fans remember: 12. On February 14, 1990, Michael scored 49 points against the Orlando Magic wearing number 12. Was there some unknown significance to that number? Nope; MJ's jersey was stolen from the locker room, and the only replacement available was a nameless number 12 jersey.

THE GREATEST TEAM OF ALL TIME

Though the flashes were there—hitting the game-winner in just his fourth game back, then scoring 55 in his next game in New York—Michael needed the 17 regular season games and a brief postseason run in 1995 to get used to basketball again. He also used that time to fuel his competitive fire.

After spending the off-season working as hard as he ever had before, MJ led the Bulls to a 72–10 record, the best in league history at the time. With new power forward Dennis Rodman grabbing all the rebounds and Michael leading the league in scoring at 30.4 points per game, the team was almost unbeatable.

In the postseason, they steamrolled their way to the Finals once again, then defeated Gary Payton and the Seattle SuperSonics in six games. MJ was named the MVP of the regular season, the All-Star Game, and the Finals.

"My attitude is that if you push me towards something that you think is a weakness, then I will turn that perceived weakness into a strength."

—Michael Jordan

MICHAEL, MEET BUGS

Always looking for another challenge to conquer, MJ next set his sights on Hollywood.

After appearing in a couple of commercials with an animated Bugs Bunny, an ambitious movie was planned that would blend live action and animation and star the two iconic pop culture figures. But not even the film's director was sure it was a good idea.

"I thought the first *Space Jam* was a silly idea," director Joe Pytka told *EW*. "I didn't know how it could become a movie [but] it did."

The plot involves Bugs and the other Looney Tunes characters needing to win a basketball game against the Monstars, and enlisting MJ to play for their team.

The film was a smash hit, opening atop the box office and over the years generating an estimated $6 billion in sales of Air Jordans, Bugs Bunny T-shirts, and other merchandise.

29

FIVE FOR FIVE

MJ and the Bulls entered the 1996 season looking to repeat as champions, after having already three-peated earlier in the decade. If Michael needed any more motivation entering the playoffs, that season's MVP award had been given to Utah's Karl Malone, despite MJ leading the Bulls to a 69–11 record.

Michael would get his shot at revenge in the NBA Finals against Malone's Jazz. He hit the game-winner at the buzzer in Game 1, then put on one of the most memorable performances in postseason history in Game 5. After winning Game 6, the Bulls were champions again.

MJ had been to the Finals five times. He was 5–0, and won five Finals MVP awards. The stage was being set for a storybook ending.

30

THE FLU GAME

MJ had the flu. He didn't have the flu. He got sick after eating a takeout pizza. He was poisoned by Jazz fans.

No matter what you believe, Michael's performance in Game 6 of the 1997 NBA Finals against the Jazz will forever be known as "The Flu Game."

Some facts seem beyond question: MJ barely slept the night before the game, suffering from flu-like symptoms. Still, knowing that a fifth championship might be hanging in the balance, he was intent on suiting up.

Michael was visibly weakened throughout the game, and the Jazz took a 16-point lead in the first half. But MJ would not be denied, chipping away at Utah's edge. At times, he needed the help of his teammates to make it back to the bench.

With the Bulls trailing by one with 46.4 seconds left, Michael made one free throw but missed the second. The Bulls controlled the rebound and got the ball back to MJ, who hit a three-pointer to seal the victory. It was yet another unforgettable performance by the G.O.A.T.

> "[I didn't] just push Scottie Pippen, Scottie Pippen pushed me. It was a big brother–little brother scenario."

—Michael Jordan

THE LAST DANCE

Everyone in the Bulls organization, from ownership to coach Phil Jackson to Michael Jordan, believed that 1997–98 would be their final season as a group. To focus his team on the challenge of achieving a second three-peat, Jackson labeled the season "The Last Dance."

Once again, MJ dominated the regular season, leading the league in scoring and winning his fifth MVP award. The Bulls reached the NBA Finals yet again and faced a rematch with the Utah Jazz.

With the Bulls tired and weakened by injuries, the series went back and forth until Game 6 in Utah. In what was possibly his last NBA game, MJ took over in the last minute, scoring a layup, stealing the ball from Karl Malone, then hitting the game-winning shot with just seconds remaining. He and the Bulls had won their sixth title, and MJ took home his sixth Finals MVP award, the most in NBA history.

It looked to be an incredible ending to an incredible career.

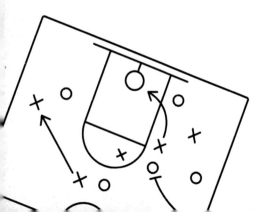

THE SHOT II

Michael's amazing career sometimes seemed like a fairy tale. So why wouldn't his final game with the Bulls have a storybook ending?

With time running out in Game 6 against Utah, MJ added one final iconic moment to his career. In honor of his series-winning shot against Cleveland years earlier, this one is known as "The Shot II."

After stealing the ball from Karl Malone on the defensive end, Michael dribbled up the court against Bryon Russell with the Bulls trailing 86–85. With under 10 seconds left in the game, MJ drove toward the free-throw line, stopped as Russell went by, then hit the championship-winning jump shot. As announcer Bob Costas said on the broadcast, "That may have been—who knows what will unfold in the next several months—but that may have been the last shot Michael Jordan will ever take in the NBA...If that's the last image of Michael Jordan, how magnificent is it?"

MJ retired, for the second time, on January 13, 1999.

> ## "Talent wins games, but teamwork and intelligence wins championships."
>
> —Michael Jordan

The City of Chicago
Congratulates the
WORLD CHAMPION -
CAGO  BULLS
ty of Chicago   Richard M. Daley, Mayor

33

A STAR AMONG STARS

Given how competitive Michael was as a player, it should come as no surprise that he saw the NBA's annual All-Star Game as another chance to prove he was the best in the game.

MJ was a 14-time All-Star, and won the game's MVP award three times, one of only six players in history to win the honor more than twice.

During the Bulls' fifth championship season, Michael became only the second player ever to win the regular season, All-Star, and Finals MVP awards in the same season.

During the 1997 game, he posted the first triple-double in the game's history, recording 14 points, 11 rebounds, and 11 assists. In his final appearance, in 2003, MJ became the game's all-time leading scorer, passing Kareem Abdul-Jabbar.

34

WHEN FIVE IS NOT ENOUGH

The NBA's MVP award is not always given to the "best" player in the league; if it was, MJ might have a dozen of the trophies on his shelf. In reality, he "only" won the award five times.

His first MVP came in 1987–88, when MJ won the Slam Dunk Contest, the All-Star Game MVP award, the Defensive Player of the Year award, and led the league in scoring. Though the Bulls were not contenders yet, his greatness could not be ignored.

After Magic Johnson won the next two awards, Michael went back-to-back in 1990 and 1991, and an argument could be made that he should have won after each full season he played until he retired following the Bulls' sixth title.

The streak was interrupted by Charles Barkley in 1993 and Karl Malone in 1996. Each time, those players met MJ in the Finals. Each time, Michael proved who the real MVP was.

THE BEST OFFENSE IS A GOOD DEFENSE

Just in case you were wondering if MJ was only good at scoring points, Michael was selected to the league's All-Defensive First Team nine times, and was the Defensive Player of the Year in 1988. During their prime years, he and Scottie Pippen formed perhaps the greatest defensive duo in league history, referred to by Bulls assistant coach Johnny Bach as the "Doberman defense."

In 1986, MJ became the first player in history to record 200 steals and 100 blocks in the same season. The year he was named DPOY, he averaged 1.6 blocks per game and an NBA-best 3.16 steals per game. He also ranks third on the NBA's all-time steals list. He did all this while often covering the opposing team's best scorer.

Lakers legend Jerry West said he appreciated MJ's defensive contributions more than his offensive ones.

"Some people want it to happen, some wish it would happen, and others make it happen."

—Michael Jordan

36

THE NEXT JORDANS

Given his revolutionary impact on the game of basketball, it was natural that people would be anxious to find the "next Jordan," someone who could take his place as the best and most popular player in the game.

Over the years, many young players tried to live up to those expectations. Some became excellent players in their own right, including Grant Hill, Vince Carter, and Jerry Stackhouse. Others struggled for a variety of reasons, such as Harold Miner, Felipe Lopez, and Ronnie Fields. But none reached the heights that Michael did.

The player who came the closest to MJ's level was Kobe Bryant, who worshipped MJ and patterned his game after him. Of their relationship, Kobe said, "We hit it off very well. He was really like a big brother, and whether it's because we see things in a similar way in terms of our competitive spirit or fire or whatever the case may be, there's an understanding that we have—a connection that we have."

"**Kobe gave every last ounce of himself to whatever he was doing.**"

—Michael Jordan

MICHAEL JORDAN... WASHINGTON WIZARD?

Perhaps everyone should have seen it coming. Still, it was hard to believe your eyes the first time Michael Jordan appeared wearing a Washington Wizards jersey.

Some background: anxious to move into the business side of the game, on January 19, 2000, MJ became part owner and president of basketball operations of the Wizards. Despite claiming he was 99.9 percent sure he would never play again, by the summer of 2001 he was feeling the itch to make another comeback.

In his first season back, injuries limited him to 60 games, during which he averaged 22.9 points per game. The following year, which everyone knew would truly be his last, he played in all 82 games despite turning 40 years old during the season. The Wizards finished each year with the identical 37–45 record.

As strange as it was to see him in a uniform that was not the Bulls', his years in Washington allowed MJ to finally retire on his own terms.

"Even when I'm old and gray, I won't be able to play it, but I'll still love the game."

—Michael Jordan

LET'S PLAY 18!

If there's anything Michael has spent more time doing in his life than playing basketball, it might be playing golf.

MJ was introduced to the sport in college when he joined teammate Buzz Peterson and future PGA pro Davis Love III on a trip to the driving range. Soon, Michael was hooked.

MJ remained a regular golfer throughout his playing career, often shooting multiple rounds of golf even before playoff games.

In 2019, Michael opened his private golf course, named The Grove XXIII (the Roman numeral stands for 23). Located in Hobe Sound, Florida, the exclusive club has fewer than 100 members and is by invitation only.

"For a competitive junkie like me, golf is a great solution because it smacks you in the face every time you think you have accomplished something," MJ said. "That to me has taken over a lot of the energy and competitiveness for basketball."

THE CALL TO THE HALL

It was a surprise to no one that MJ was selected to join the Naismith Memorial Basketball Hall of Fame as soon as he was eligible. The ceremony was held on September 11, 2009, in Springfield, Massachusetts. Joining MJ's Hall of Fame class that year were Dream Team teammates John Stockton and David Robinson, Jerry Sloan, and C. Vivian Stringer.

With former teammates, family, and friends in the audience, the speech he gave that night was classic MJ: he talked about the things that motivated him, such as being "cut" from his high school team and being frozen out during his first All-Star Game. But he also showed fans an emotional side, crying as he spoke about how much the honor meant to him.

"Although I'm recognized with this tremendous honor of being in the basketball Hall of Fame," he said, "I don't look at this moment as a defining end to my relationship with the game of basketball. It's simply a continuation of something that I started a long time ago. One day you might look up and see me playing the game at 50. Oh, don't laugh. Never say never. Because limits, like fears, are often just an illusion."

MICHAEL'S HORNETS

MJ was a one-of-a-kind basketball player, so why shouldn't he be the same type of owner?

In 2006, Michael bought a minority ownership in the Charlotte Bobcats, and four years later became the majority owner. The move made him the first former player to own an NBA team and the league's first Black owner.

"Purchasing the Bobcats is the culmination of my post-playing career goal of becoming the majority owner of an NBA franchise," MJ said in a statement. "I am especially pleased to have the opportunity to build a winning team in my home state of North Carolina. I plan to make this franchise an organization that Charlotte can be proud of, and I am committed to doing all that I can to achieve this goal."

The Bobcats were officially renamed the Hornets in 2014. Though the team hasn't had much playoff success during Michael's tenure, fans can rest assured that they have an owner who will do everything he can to win.